I Have Who Has

3 - 5 years

Language and cognitive development

Copyright © 2022 by A Devi Thangamaniam.

All right reserved. No part of this publication may be reproduced, distributed, or transmitted in any form or by any means, including photocopying, recording, or other electronic or mechanical methods, without the prior written permission of the author, except in the case of brief quotations embodied in critical reviews and certain other non-commercial uses permitted by copyright law.

Information: MiLu Children's Educational Source.
www.my-willing.com
ISBN: 979 8 88627 088 4

I Have

Who Has

The Play is a Fun

Let's Play Begin

 I have an apple.

Keep it in a couple.

Who has a banana?

 The bird has a banana.

 The bird has a banana.
It plays with Zanana.

Who has a duck?

 The truck has a duck.

The truck has a duck.

The duck sound is quack.

Who has a mango?

 The pig has a mango.

The pig has a mango.

You win game a bingo.

Who has a pear?

 The bear has a pear.

The bear has a pear.

The shoes for wear.

Who has a star?

 The car has a star.

The car has a star.

Tia's dad is there.

Who has a house?

 The mouse has a house.

The mouse has a house.

My mom wears a blouse.

Who has a ball?

 The dog has a ball.

The dog has a ball.

The tree is too tall.

Who has a bug?

 The cup has a bug.

The cup has a bug.

You give me a hug.

Who has a pail?

 The pencil has a pail.

The pencil has a pail.
Cut your long nail.

Who has a rabbit?

 The butterfly has a rabbit.

The butterfly has a rabbit.
Please move a little bit.

Who has a carrot?

 The parrot has a carrot.

The parrot has a carrot.

He screeches like a parrot.

Who has a shirt?

 The heart has a shirt.

The heart has a shirt.

Her sister wears a skirt.

Who has a crow?

 The boat has a crow.

The boat has a crow.

Please push my wheelbarrow.

Who has a frock?

 The girl has a frock.

The girl has a frock.

They jump like a frog.

Who has a bus?

 The boy has a bus.

The boy has a bus.

You are my precious.

Who has a flower?

The dinosaur has a flower.

The dinosaur has a flower.

The snail crawls slower.

Who has ice cream?

 The orange has ice cream.

The orange has ice cream.
Use to eat less butter cream.

Who has a hat?

 The cat has a hat.

The cat has a hat.
You sit on a mat.

Who has a dish?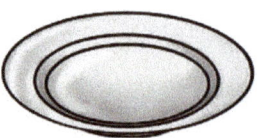

 The fish has a dish.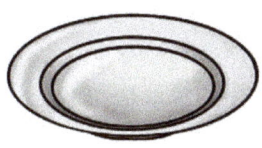

The fish has a dish.

The tank full of fish.

Who has a spoon?

 The bottle has a spoon.

The bottle has a spoon.

You cut hair at a salon.

Who has a plane?

 The violin has a plane.

The violin has a plane.

Fly like a super plane.

Who has a stick?

 The chick has a stick.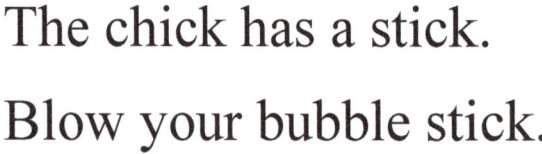

The chick has a stick.

Blow your bubble stick.

Who has an oil lamp?

 The triangle has an oil lamp.

The triangle has an oil lamp.

Fun in the summer camp.

Who has a circle?

 The clock has a circle.

The clock has a circle.

He rides on a bicycle.

Who has a strawberry?

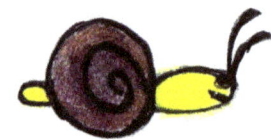 The snail has a strawberry.

The snail has a strawberry.
You drink juice cranberry.

Who has a mitten?

 The leaf has a mitten.

The leaf has a mitten.
Arrange colour with a pattern.

Who has a kite?

 The bicycle has a kite.

The bicycle has a kite.

The snow is white.

Who has a rat?

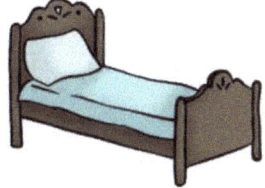 The bed has a rat.

The bed has a rat.

We sit on a mat.

Who has played this?

We played this.

Have more fun.

The play is done.

www.ingramcontent.com/pod-product-compliance
Lightning Source LLC
LaVergne TN
LVHW072133060526
838201LV00072B/5024